Working with Words

Written by Sue Lewis and Amy Stern

Editor: Vicky Shiotsu
Illustrator: Terri Rae
Cover Illustrator: Tim Huhn
Designer: Karen Hanke
Cover Designer: Barbara Peterson
Art Director: Tom Cochrane
Project Director: Carolea Williams

Table of Contents

Introduction

The 14 different *Working with Words* centers presented in this book give students many opportunities to manipulate letters and words. Each center is designed to reinforce literacy skills as students work together with partners or in small groups.

Literacy centers allow students to work independently to extend the concepts they have learned during classroom instruction. Literacy centers also give teachers greater flexibility, permitting them to work with individuals or small groups while the rest of the students are actively involved in constructive activities. Word work literacy centers, in particular, help early emergent and emergent readers develop phonemic awareness, word patterning, and sight word recognition, all of which work together to further their ability to read independently.

While literacy centers are effective in increasing students' language skills, we know that it takes time and effort to prepare for them every week. For example, appropriate pictures have to be collected, word cards made, and reproducible pages developed. *Working with Words* provides ready-to-go materials that let you create centers almost instantly. For many of the centers, all you need to do is reproduce some cards (featuring letters, words, or pictures) and cut them out.

Center Activities

Each activity has been kept simple to assure that students readily understand what to do after a brief explanation from you. Each center includes:
- an introductory page that explains how to assemble and use the center
- cards, game boards, and/or reproducible activity sheets to be used at the center

Storage

Once you reproduce and cut out the materials for each center, place each set in a resealable plastic bag. Write the name of the activity on the bag with a permanent marker, then store all the bags in one box.

A Word About Paper

We suggest that you use tagboard or cover stock for reproducing the cards needed for each literacy center. Tagboard is sturdier than ordinary photocopy paper. Many schools carry colored tagboard that can be run through a copy machine. If you wish, reproduce the cards on different-colored paper for each center. That will make it easy to distinguish the different sets. (If you do not have colored tagboard or cover stock at school, you can find it at most office supply stores or copy shops.) Choose lighter shades so that the print will show up well. If you have time, before cutting out the cards, laminate the tagboard to increase its durability.

High Frequency Words

Purpose

Students create a portable word chart that matches the class word wall. This word chart will help students with their reading and writing at home as well as at school. It can also serve as an easy-to-use dictionary.

Materials Included

- Word chart letters
- High frequency word list (for teacher reference)

Materials Needed

- File folders (one per child)
- Scissors and stapler

Optional Materials

- Crayons

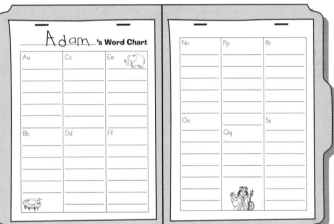

Directions to the Teacher

1. Reproduce a set of word chart letters for each student. Staple the word chart letter pages to the inside of each file folder. Staple two pages on the left and two pages on the right.

2. As words are added to the class word wall, have students write the words on their personal word charts. They can use the words to write sentences or stories at the word work center.

3. Students may choose to use crayons to highlight the high frequency words in the same color as the paper on which the classroom wall words are written.

_____'s **Word Chart**

Aa	Cc	Ee
Bb	Dd	Ff

Gg

_____

_____

_____

_____

Hh

_____

_____

_____

_____

Ii

_____

Jj

_____

_____

_____

Kk

_____

_____

_____

_____

Ll

_____

_____

_____

_____

Mm

_____

_____

_____

_____

Nn

_____

_____

_____

_____

_____

Oo

_____

_____

_____

_____

_____

Pp

_____

_____

_____

_____

_____

Qq

_____

_____

_____

Rr

_____

_____

_____

_____

Ss

_____

_____

_____

_____

Tt

Uu

Vv

Ww

Xx

Yy

Zz

High Frequency Words

Kindergarten Words	on	day	out
am	or	down	over
an	said	each	part
and	see	find	she
are	that	first	so
as	the	get	some
at	they	had	take
be	this	has	than
can	to	her	their
did	up	him	them
do	was	how	then
for	with	if	there
from	yes	into	these
go	you	its	time
have		long	two
he		look	use
his	**1st Grade Words**	made	way
I	about	make	we
in	all	many	were
is	been	may	what
it	but	more	when
like	by	new	which
me	call	no	who
my	come	now	will
not	could	one	word
of		only	would
		other	your

Letter Recognition

Purpose
Students match letters and/or letters and pictures that begin with the same sound.

Materials Included
- Set of capital letter cards
- Set of lowercase letter cards
- Set of 31 picture cards
  (one picture for the beginning sound of each letter of the alphabet, plus one for each short vowel)

Materials Needed
- Scissors
- Plastic resealable bags

Optional Materials
- Tagboard and laminating machine

Directions to the Teacher

Reproduce the letter and picture cards on white or colored card stock, laminate, and cut out. Place 6 to 12 letter and/or picture pairs in a bag (e.g., AA, BB, CC; or Aa, Bb, Cc, or A apron, B bear, C cat). Several letter recognition activities can be played:

1. Students match capital letters to each other. B B
2. Students match lowercase letters to each other. b b
3. Students match capital and lowercase letters. B b
4. Students match letters to pictures by listening to the beginning sound.
5. Students turn cards facedown and choose two cards per turn. They look for pairs of letters or pairs of letters and pictures to play a memory match game.

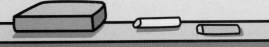

Alphabet Cards for Letter Recognition

One picture per letter,
plus five extra short vowel pictures

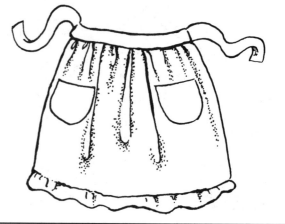

Working with Words © 2001 Creative Teaching Press

14   Letter Recognition

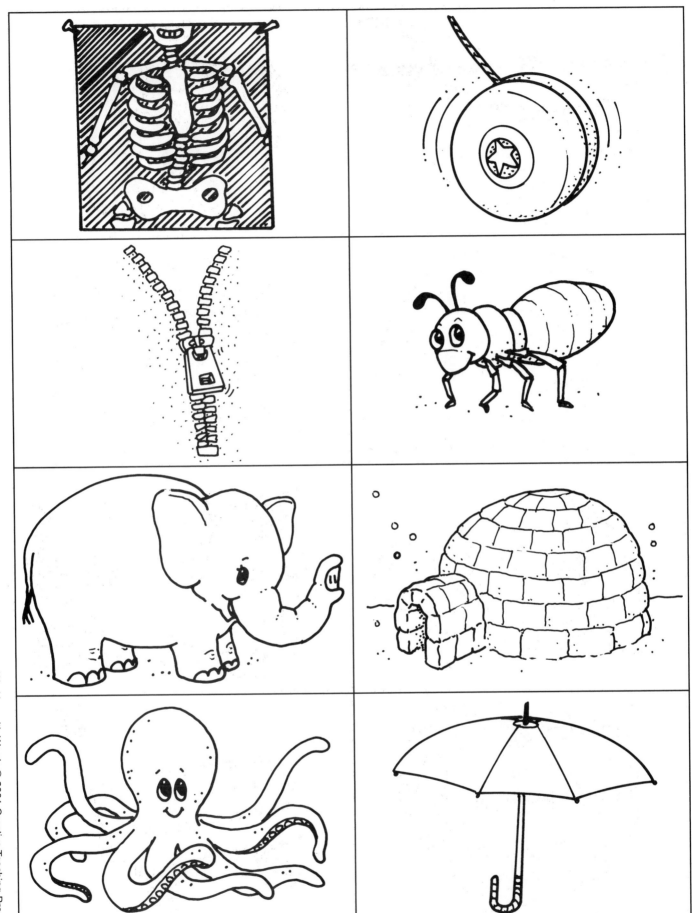

G →	D →	A →
g →	d →	a →
H →	E →	B →
h →	e →	b →
I →	F →	C →
i →	f →	c →

→ P	→ M	→ J
→ p	→ m	→ j
→ Q	→ N	→ K
→ q	→ n	→ k
→ R	→ O	→ L
→ r	→ o	→ l

Y →	V →	S →
y →	v →	s →
Z →	W →	T →
z →	w →	t →
→	X →	U →
→	x →	u →

Onsets and Rimes

Purpose

Onsets and rimes are used to help students see patterns and pronounce unfamiliar words. This center includes materials that will help students reinforce their ability to work with onsets and rimes.

Materials Included

- Letter strips with onsets
- 16 rime cards

Materials Needed

- Scissors

Optional Materials

- Tagboard
- Laminating machine

Directions to the Teacher

Reproduce the onset strips and the rime cards on white or colored tagboard, laminate, and cut out. Cut two small slits along the dotted lines in each rime card. Run the onset strip through the slits. Students read the words to a partner and write down the words they discover.

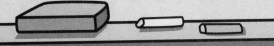

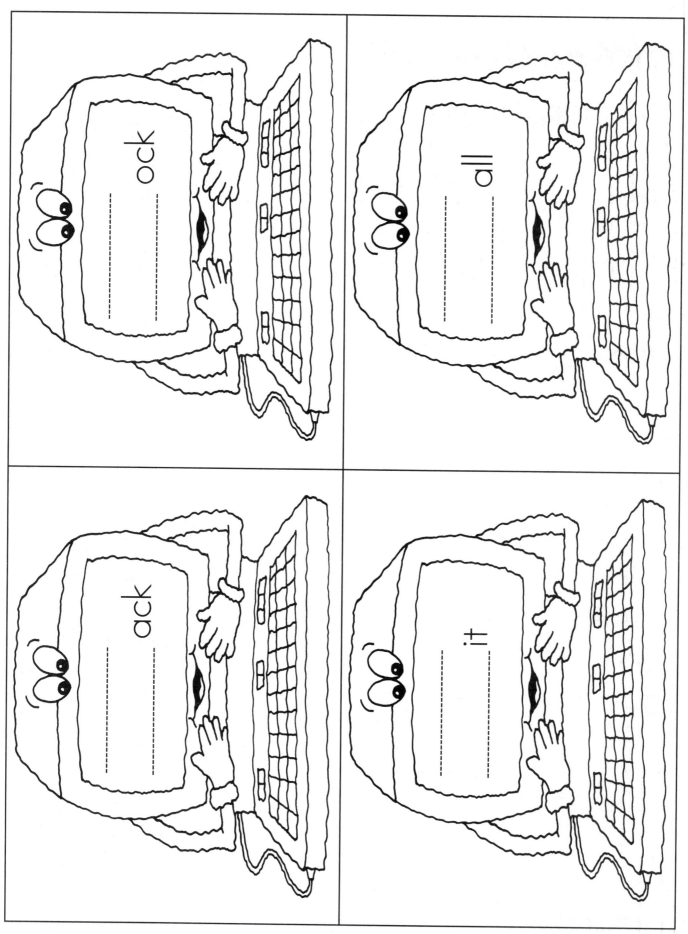

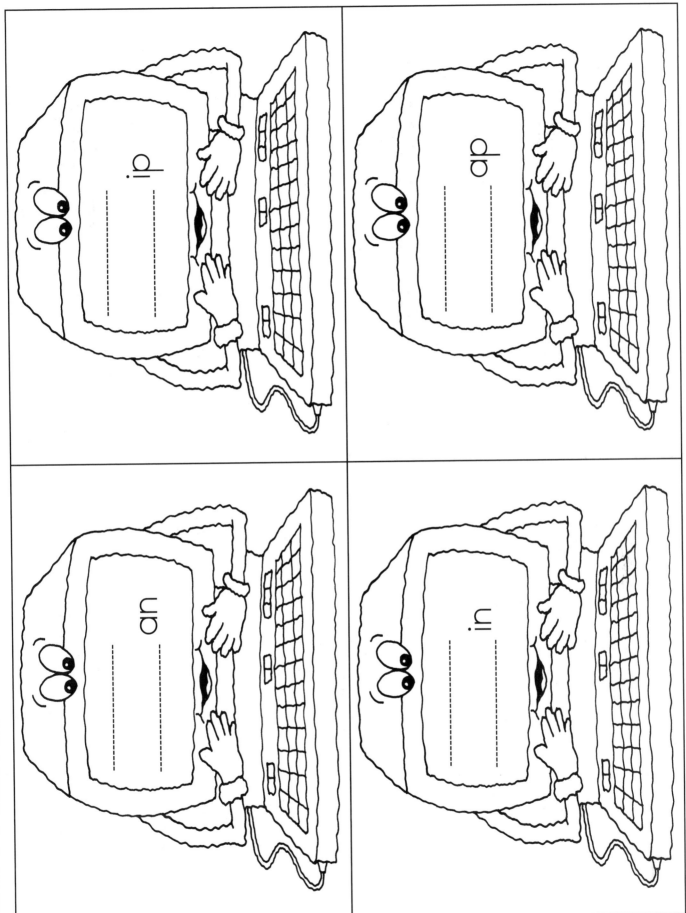

ig

op

ot

at

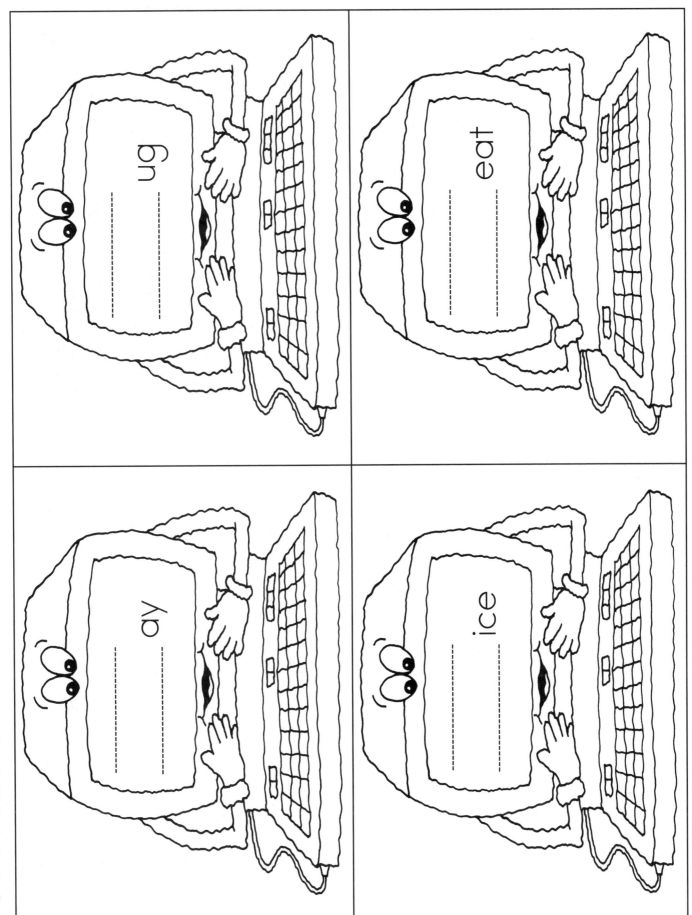

start	start	start	start	start	start
b	b	b	b	b	b
c	c	c	c	c	c
d	d	d	d	d	d
f	f	f	f	f	f
h	h	h	h	h	h
l	l	l	l	l	l
m	m	m	m	m	m
n	n	n	n	n	n
p	p	p	p	p	p
r	r	r	r	r	r
s	s	s	s	s	s
t	t	t	t	t	t
w	w	w	w	w	w
stop	stop	stop	stop	stop	stop

Rhyming Words

Purpose
Students pair rhyming words.

Materials Included
- 15 pairs of rhyming word cards

Materials Needed
- Scissors

Optional Materials
- Tagboard
- Laminating machine

Directions to the Teacher

Reproduce the picture cards on white or colored tagboard, laminate, and cut out. Spread the cards faceup on a table. Each student selects a card, reads his or her word aloud to a partner, and finds the matching rhyming word.

Variation
Have students list additional words that rhyme with the rhyming word pair.

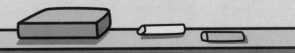

hat

cat

flag

bag

fan

man

pen

hen

bell

well

pig

wig

stick

chick

clock

sock

fox

box

Working with Words © 2001 Creative Teaching Press

dog

frog

sun

run

rug

bug

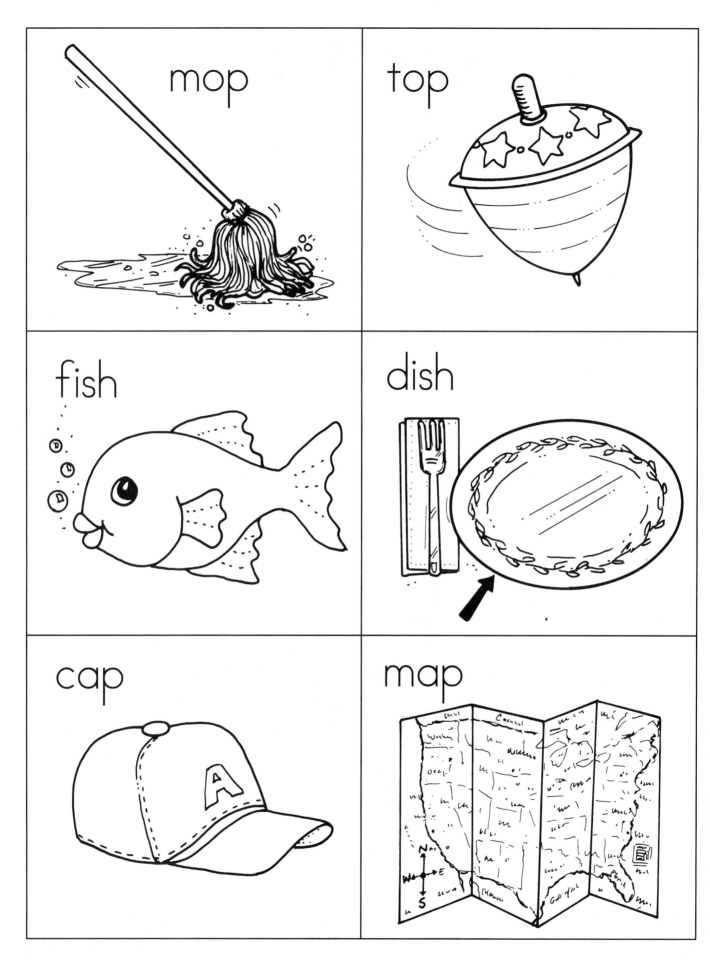

mop

top

fish

dish

cap

map

ABC Order

Purpose
Students place letters in ABC order.

Materials Included
• Capital and lowercase letter cards

Materials Needed
• Scissors

Optional Materials
• Tagboard
• Laminating machine
• Paper clips, string, and dowels or pencils
• Magnets (one per "pole")

Directions to the Teacher

Reproduce the fish-shaped letter cards on white or colored tagboard, laminate, and cut out. Place all the fish cards facedown on a flat surface. Have students "fish" out 4 to 6 letters at a time and put them in alphabetical order. Add more letters as students become more proficient.

Variations
Place a paper clip on the edge of each fish card. Tie a piece of string and a magnet to the end of dowels or pencils. Have students "fish" out the letters using their "fishing poles." Use the blank fish to write words that students can place in alphabetical order.

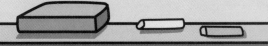

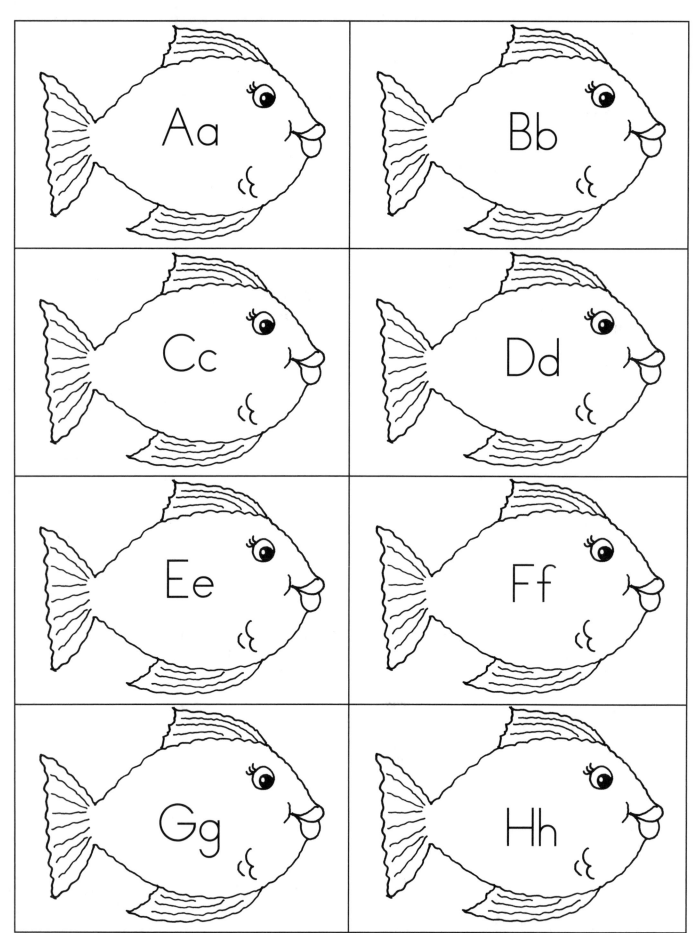

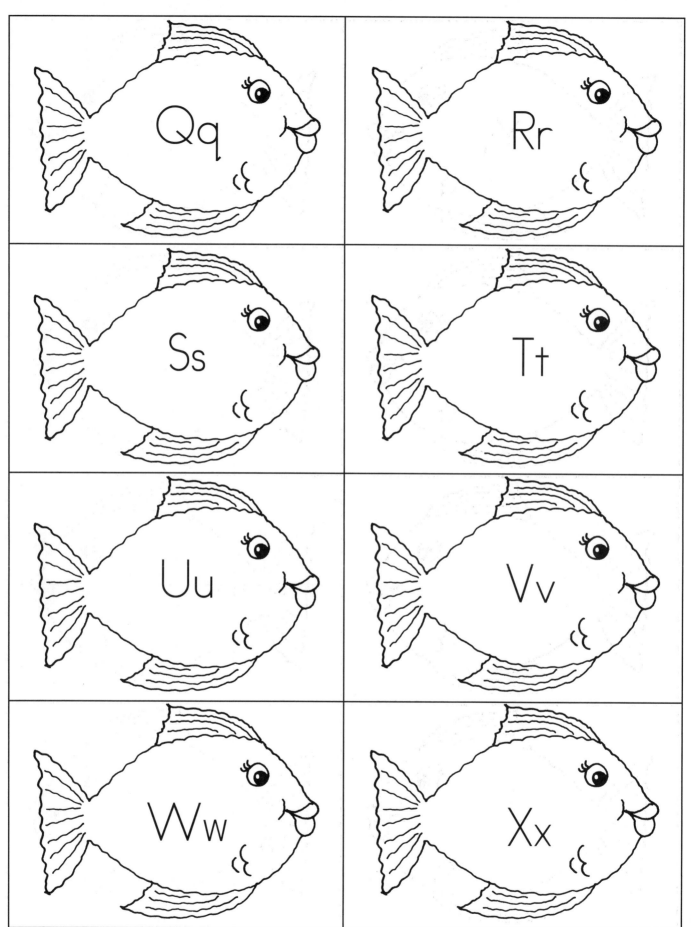

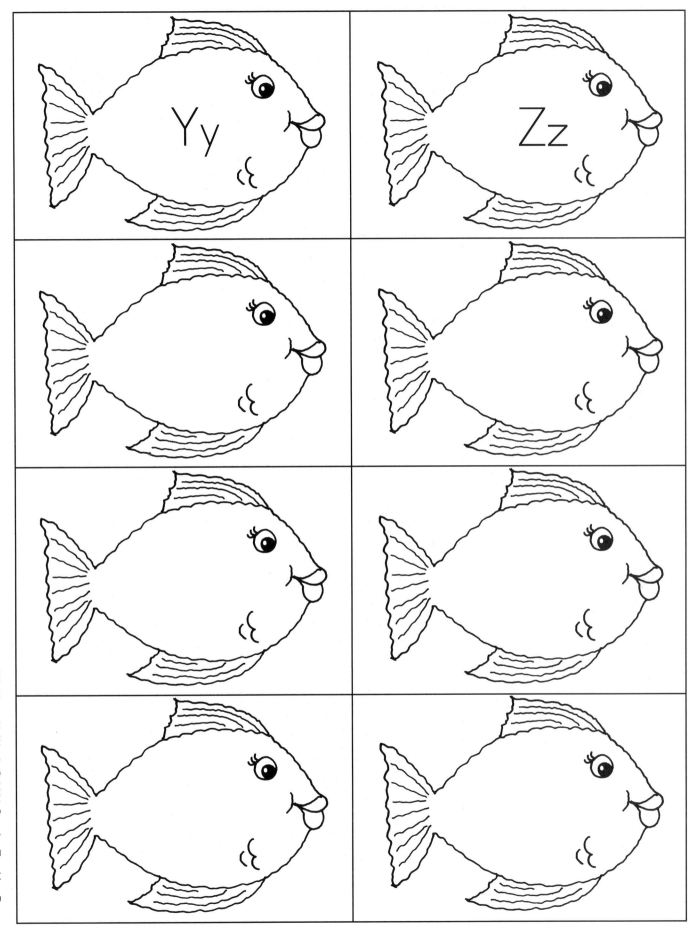

Printing Practice Using High Frequency Words

Purpose

Students gain printing skills as they practice the spelling of high frequency words.

Materials Included

- Reproducible printing practice pages

Materials Needed

- Pencils

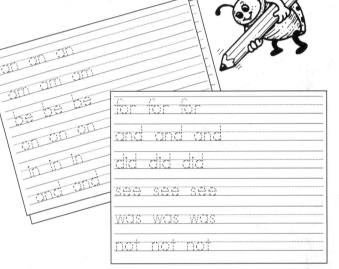

Directions to the Teacher

Reproduce several sheets at a time, and place them in the literacy center for students to use. Have students trace and write the high frequency words.

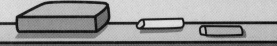

for for for

his his his

did did did

she she she

was was was

not not not

have have

said said

like like

with with

they they

this this

but but

come come

made made

one one

look look

she she

Beginning Consonants Game

Purpose
Students identify beginning consonant sounds.

Materials Included
- Beginning Consonants game board
- Set of 36 picture cards
- Beginning Consonants reference card

Materials Needed
- File folder
- Glue
- Scissors
- Die
- Game markers

Optional Materials
- Tagboard
- Laminating machine

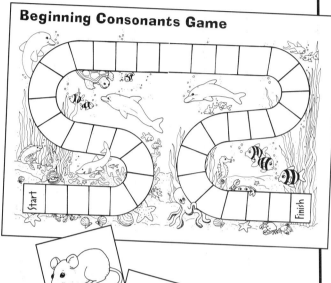

Beginning Consonants Game

Directions to the Teacher

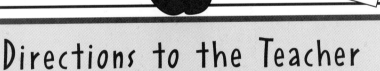

Glue the game board into a file folder and laminate for greater durability. Reproduce the picture cards on white or colored tagboard, laminate, and cut out.

Give students the following instructions:

1. Place the game markers on Start. Place the picture cards facedown in a pile.

2. The first player picks up a card and names the picture. He or she then names the beginning consonant. If correct, the player rolls the die and moves his or her game piece that many spaces on the game board. If incorrect, the player does not move for that turn. (Players may refer to the reference card on page 49 to check their answers.)

3. Players who land on a specially marked space can move an extra space by saying another word or words beginning with the consonant just named.

4. Players take turns picking up cards and naming the beginning consonants. The first player to reach Finish wins.

Beginning Consonants Game

Say a word that begins with the consonant just named. Move an extra space.

Say a word that begins with the consonant just named. Move an extra space.

Start

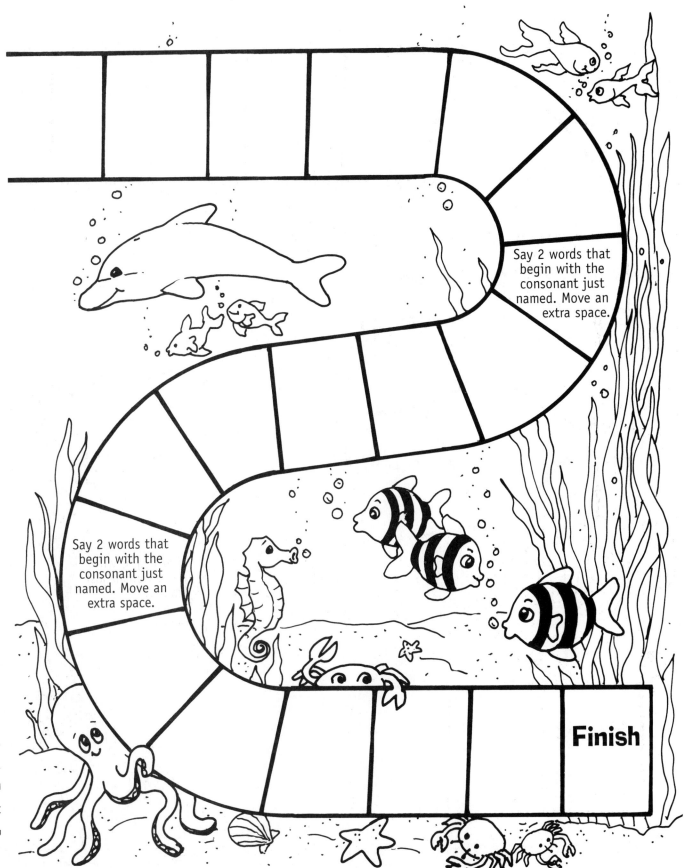

Say 2 words that begin with the consonant just named. Move an extra space.

Say 2 words that begin with the consonant just named. Move an extra space.

Finish

Beginning Consonants Game

Beginning Consonants Reference Card

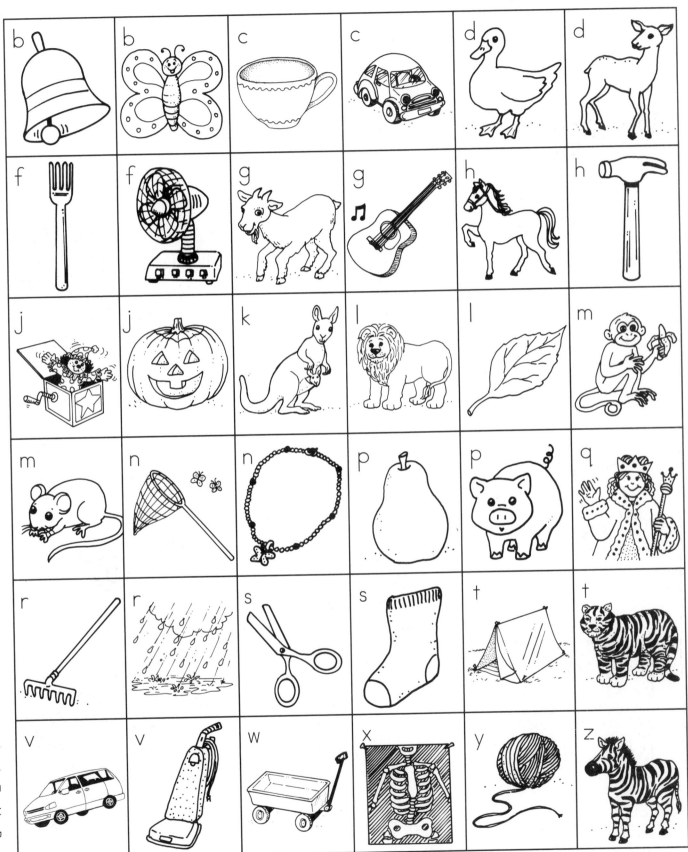

Working with Words © 2001 Creative Teaching Press

Short Vowels Lotto

Purpose
Students identify short vowel sounds in the middle of words.

Materials Included
- Lotto game board
- Set of 48 picture cards
- Short Vowels reference card

Materials Needed
- Scissors
- Paper bag

Optional Materials
- Tagboard
- Laminating machine

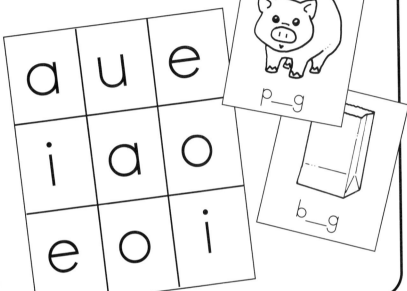

Directions to the Teacher

Reproduce one lotto game board for each child. Reproduce the picture cards on white or colored tagboard, laminate, and cut out.

Give students the following instructions:

1. Each player gets a lotto game board and writes a vowel in each space. Vowels may be written up to two times on one board.

2. Place the picture cards inside a paper bag.

3. The first player draws a card from the bag, says the name of the picture, and names the missing vowel. If the player has a matching vowel on his or her lotto game board, he or she places the picture card over it. If not, the player sets the picture card aside. (Players may refer to the reference card on page 56 to check their answers.)

4. Players take turns. The first player to cover all the letters on his or her lotto board wins the game.

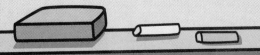

Lotto Game Board

b__g

b__t

c__n

c__p

c__t

f__n

h__t

l__mp

m__sk

r__t

b__d

b__ll

d__sk

h__n

n__st

p__n

t__nt	v__st	w__b	b__b
d__sh	f__sh	h__ll	ch__n
p__g	p__n	w__g	l__p
b__x	d__g	d__ll	f__x

l__ck

l_g

p__t

r__ck

s__ck

t_p

b__g

b__s

c__p

d__ck

g__m

c__t

pl__g

r__g

s__n

t__b

Short Vowels Reference Card

b<u>a</u>g	b<u>a</u>t	c<u>a</u>n	c<u>a</u>p	c<u>a</u>t	f<u>a</u>n	h<u>a</u>t
l<u>a</u>mp	m<u>a</u>sk	r<u>a</u>t	b<u>e</u>d	b<u>e</u>ll	d<u>e</u>sk	h<u>e</u>n
n<u>e</u>st	p<u>e</u>n	t<u>e</u>nt	v<u>e</u>st	w<u>e</u>b	b<u>i</u>b	d<u>i</u>sh
f<u>i</u>sh	h<u>i</u>ll	ch<u>i</u>n	p<u>i</u>g	p<u>i</u>n	w<u>i</u>g	l<u>i</u>p
b<u>o</u>x	d<u>o</u>g	d<u>o</u>ll	f<u>o</u>x	l<u>o</u>ck	l<u>o</u>g	p<u>o</u>t
r<u>o</u>ck	s<u>o</u>ck	t<u>o</u>p	b<u>u</u>g	b<u>u</u>s	c<u>u</u>p	d<u>u</u>ck
g<u>u</u>m	c<u>u</u>t	pl<u>u</u>g	r<u>u</u>g	s<u>u</u>n	t<u>u</u>b	

Beginning Blends Race

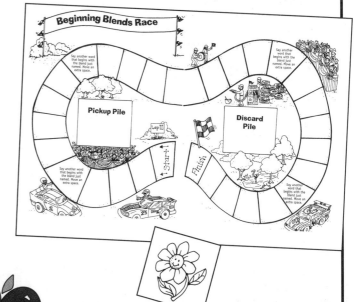

Purpose

Students identify beginning consonant blends.

Materials Included

- Beginning Blends Race game board
- Set of 48 picture cards
- Consonant Blends reference card

Materials Needed

- File folder
- Glue
- Scissors
- Die
- Game markers

Optional Materials

- Tagboard and laminating machine

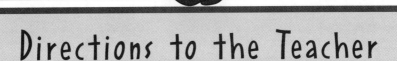

Directions to the Teacher

Glue the game board into a file folder and laminate for greater durability. Reproduce the picture cards on white or colored tagboard, laminate, and cut out.

Give students the following instructions:

1. Place the game markers on Start and the picture cards facedown on the space marked Pickup Pile.

2. The first player picks up a card and names the picture. He or she then names the consonant blend letters heard at the beginning of the word. If correct, the player rolls the die and moves his or her game piece that many spaces on the game board. If incorrect, the player does not move for that turn. The player places the card facedown on the game board in the discard pile. (Players may refer to the reference card on page 64 to check their answers.)

3. Players who land on a specially marked space can move an extra space by saying another word that begins with the consonant blend just named.

4. Players take turns picking up cards and naming the consonant blends. The first player to reach Finish wins.

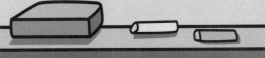

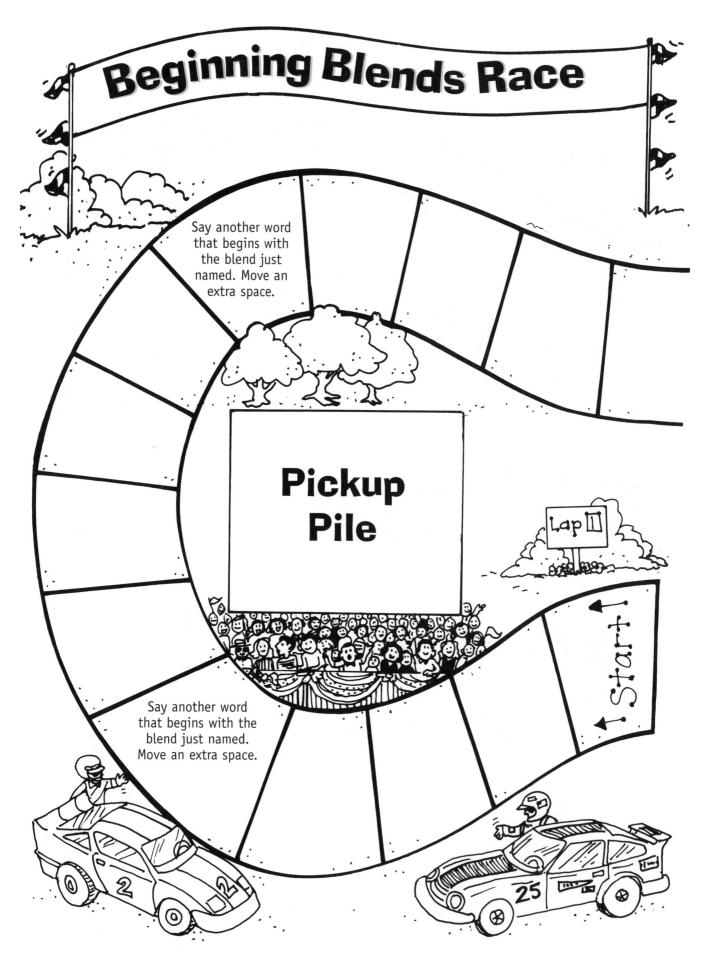

Beginning Blends Race

Say another word that begins with the blend just named. Move an extra space.

Pickup Pile

Lap II

Start

Say another word that begins with the blend just named. Move an extra space.

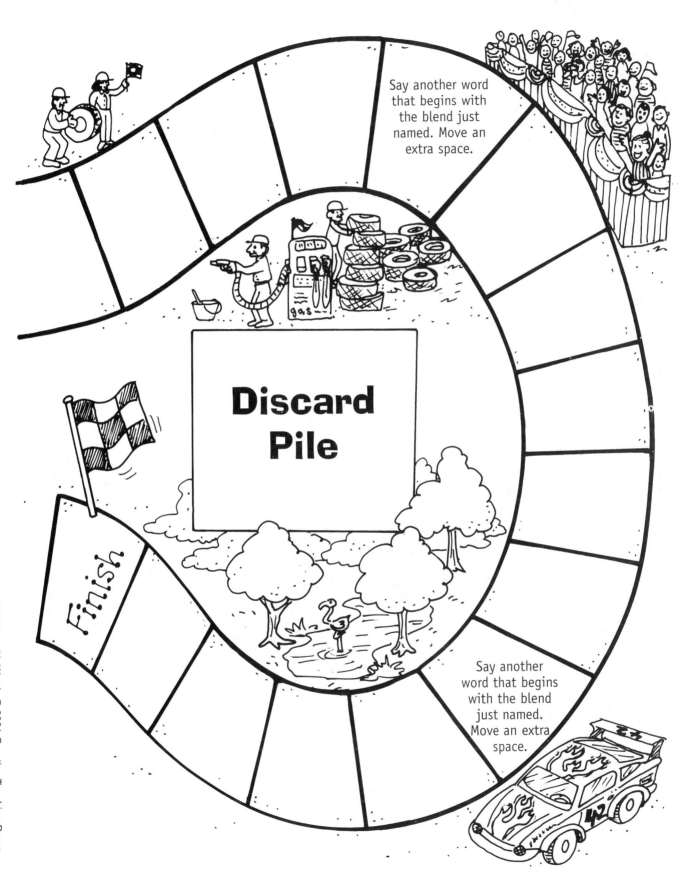

Say another word that begins with the blend just named. Move an extra space.

Discard Pile

Finish

Say another word that begins with the blend just named. Move an extra space.

Beginning Blends Race

Beginning Blends Reference Card

bl	bl	br	br	cl	cl	cl
cr	cr	cr	dr	dr	fl	fl
fl	fr	fr	gl	gl	gr	gr
pl	pl	pl	pr	pr	sk	sk
sk	sl	sl	sl	sm	sm	sn
sn	sn	sp	sp	st	st	st
sw	sw	sw	tr	tr	tr	

Onsets and Rimes Word Game

Purpose
Students form words with combinations of onsets and rimes.

Materials Included
- 40 onset cards
- 36 rime cards

Materials Needed
- Scissors
- Lined paper

Optional Materials
- Glue
- Tagboard
- Laminating machine

Directions to the Teacher

Reproduce the onset cards and rime cards on white or colored tagboard, laminate, and cut out.

Give students the following instructions:

1. Work in groups of twos or threes.
2. Together, players select one rime card and lay it in front of them. The onset cards are shuffled and placed facedown.
3. Students take turns picking up an onset card and placing it in front of the rime card. If a word is made, the student keeps the onset card. If not, the card is set aside.
4. When all the onset cards have been picked up, the student with the most cards wins.

For a follow-up, students lay out all the onset cards that made words with a rime card, then write the words on lined paper or in their word charts.

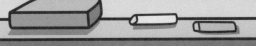

Working with Words © 2001 Creative Teaching Press

b	c	d	f
g	h	j	k
l	m	n	p
r	s	t	v

w	bl	br
cl	cr	dr
fl	fr	gl
gr	pl	pr

qu	sk	sl
sm	sn	sp
st	tr	ch
sh	th	wh

_ake

_ale

_all

_ack

_ail

_ain

ar

at

ate

an

ank

ap

_est

.ice

.ick

_ay

_eat

_ell

.ine ___

.ing ___

.ink ___

.ide ___

.ill ___

.in ___

ock ___

oke ___

op ___

ip ___

it ___

ame ___

_ug

_unk

_un

_ore

_ot

_ump

Ending Consonants Memory Match

Purpose
This center reinforces ending consonant sounds and memory skills.

Materials Included
• Set of 24 picture cards
• Ending Consonants reference card

Materials Needed
• Scissors

Optional Materials
• Tagboard
• Laminating machine

Directions to the Teacher

Reproduce the picture cards on white or colored tagboard, laminate, and cut them out.

Give students the following instructions:

1. Shuffle the cards and lay them facedown.
2. The first player picks up two cards, names the pictures, and states the ending consonant of each word. If the consonants match, the player keeps the cards. If not, the player returns them facedown to their original positions. (Players may refer to the reference card on page 78 to check the answer.)
3. The game continues with players taking turns picking up two cards at a time.
4. When all the cards have been picked up, the player with the most cards wins.

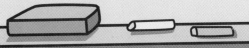

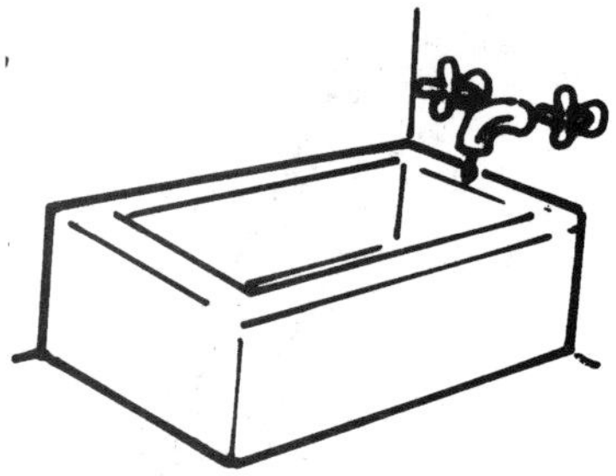

tu___

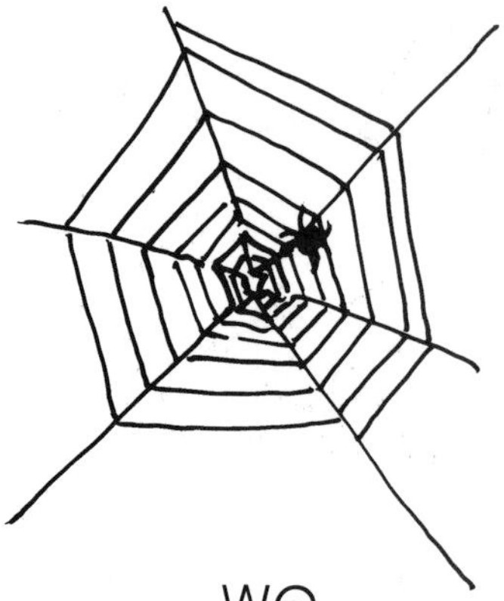

we___

be___

bir___

lea___

roo___

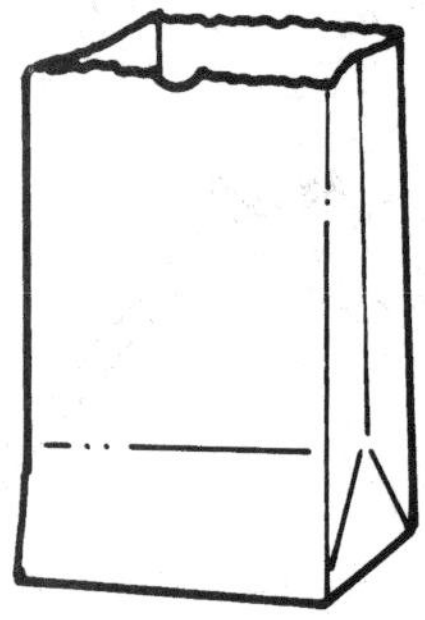

ba___

pi___

sea___

tai___

broo___

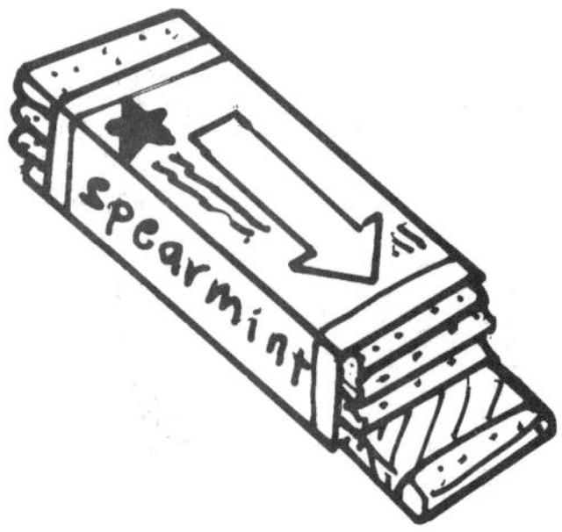

gu___

fa___

he___

pi___

su___

cu___

to___

ca___

goa___

ne___

po___

fo___

si___

Ending Consonants Reference Card

tu**b**	we**b**	be**d**	bir**d**
lea**f**	roo**f**	ba**g**	pi**g**
sea**l**	tai**l**	broo**m**	gu**m**
fa**n**	he**n**	**p**i**n**	su**n**
cu**p**	to**p**	**c**a**t**	goa**t**
ne**t**	**p**o**t**	fo**x**	si**x**

Beginning Consonants Sort

Purpose

Students sort pictures and high frequency words by their beginning consonants.

Materials Included

- Set of 36 picture cards on pages 46–48
- Set of 20 consonant cards
- Set of 54 word cards

Materials Needed

- Scissors
- Plastic resealable bags

Optional Materials

- Tagboard
- Laminating machine

Directions to the Teacher

1. Duplicate the letter cards, word cards, and picture cards on tagboard. Laminate and cut them out. Decide on doing a picture sort, word sort, or both.

2. Have students place 3 to 5 letter cards of their choice across the top of the table.

3. Under each letter, have them place the picture cards and/or word cards that start with the appropriate consonant.

4. As a follow-up, students create their own sorting rule.

Note: If students are matching letters to picture cards, encourage them to look at both the beginning and ending sound of the word.

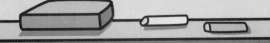

b	c	d	f
g	h	j	k
l	m	n	p
q	r	s	t
v	w	y	z

Words to match picture cards	fork
bell	fan
butterfly	goat
cup	guitar
car	horse
duck	hammer
deer	jack-in-the-box

jack-o'-lantern	necklace
kangaroo	pear
lion	pig
leaf	queen
monkey	rake
mouse	rain
net	scissors

sock	yarn
tent	zebra
tiger	**Decodable Words**
van	but
vacuum	can
wagon	cat
x-ray	did

get	got
him	had
top	man
not	sun
sit	will
pup	hot
yes	big

Working with Words © 2001 Creative Teaching Press

Beginning Blends Sort

Purpose

Students sort pictures and high frequency words by their beginning consonant blend.

Materials Included

- Set of 48 picture cards on pages 60–63
- Set of 19 consonant blend cards
- Set of 54 word cards

Materials Needed

- Scissors
- Plastic resealable bag

Optional Materials

- Tagboard
- Laminating machine

Directions to the Teacher

1. Duplicate the blends cards, word cards, and picture cards on white or colored tagboard. Laminate and cut out. Decide if you will have students do a picture sort, word sort, or both.

2. Have students place 3 to 5 blends cards of their choice across the top of the table.

3. Under each card, have them place the picture cards and/or word cards that start with the appropriate beginning blend sound.

4. As a follow-up, students can create their own sorting rule.

Note: If students are matching letters to picture cards, encourage them to look at both the beginning and ending sound of the word.

bl	fl	pr	sp
br	fr	sk	st
cl	gl	sl	sw
cr	gr	sm	tr
dr	pl	sn	

Words to match Beginning Blends picture cards	clown
block	crown
blanket	crab
broom	crayon
brush	dress
clock	drum
clothes	flag

Working with Words © 2001 Creative Teaching Press

flower	grapes
fly	plane
frog	plug
fruit	plant
glass	price
globe	present
grass	skunk

skirt	snake
skate	snail
sled	snowman
slide	spider
slippers	spoon
smoke	stamp
smile	stove

star	**More Blend Words**
swing	clap
swan	black
sweater	slip
tree	trap
truck	swim
triangle	plum

Working with Words © 2001 Creative Teaching Press

Short Vowel Sort

Purpose

Students sort pictures and words by their short vowel sound.

Materials Included

- Set of 48 picture cards on pages 53–55
- Set of 10 short vowel cards
- Set of 61 word cards

Materials Needed

- Scissors
- Plastic resealable bags

Optional Materials

- Tagboard and laminating machine

Directions to the Teacher

1. Duplicate the letter cards, word cards, and picture cards on white or colored tagboard. Laminate and cut out. Decide if you will have students do a picture sort, word sort, or both.

2. Have students place five vowel cards (a, e, i, o, u) across the top of the table.

3. Under each letter, have them place the picture or word cards that contain the matching short vowel.

4. As a follow-up, students can create their own sorting rule.

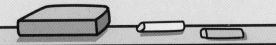

a	a	**Words to match short vowel picture cards**
e	e	bag
		bat
i	i	can
o	o	cap
		cat
u	u	fan

Working with Words © 2001 Creative Teaching Press

hat	hen
lamp	nest
mask	pen
rat	tent
bed	vest
bell	web
desk	bib

dish	lip
fish	box
hill	dog
chin	doll
pig	fox
pin	lock
wig	log

Working with Words © 2001 Creative Teaching Press

pot	duck
rock	gum
sock	cut
top	plug
bug	rug
bus	sun
cup	tub

Additional short vowel words	get
at	sit
end	hop
in	bun
on	ham
up	fun
sat	tap